THE BIRMINGHAM SCRAPBOOK

VOL 2

Alton & Jo Douglas

Work continues on the Inner Ring Road, February 1959. The Scala cinema is on the right.

© 2006 Alton and Jo Douglas
ISBN 1 85858 295 4
Published by Brewin Books Ltd., Doric House, 56 Alcester Road, Studley, Warwickshire B80 7LG.
Printed by Warwick Printing Co. Ltd., Caswell Road, Leamington Spa CV31 1QD.
Layout by Alton and Jo Douglas

Albert Street, January 1960.

Front Cover: Something must have been on special offer! The Rag Market, 4th September 1956.

Contents

Page 4   Early Years

Page 13   1900

Page 21   1910

Page 35   1920

Page 50   1930

Page 69   1940

Page 81   1950

Page 90   1960

Page 100   Acknowledgements

BREWIN BOOKS LTD

Doric House, 56 Alcester Road,
Studley, Warwickshire B80 7LG

Tel: 01527 854228 Fax: 01527 852746
Email: enquiries@brewinbooks.com

Vat Registration No. 705 0077 73

Dear Nostalgic,

To produce a successful pictorial book you really do need to have big ears – well, the ability to listen anyway! Most of the comments about "The Birmingham Scrapbook Vol 1" seemed to relate to the more historic items so, although this edition stretches from 1867 to 1969, the bulk of the material comes under the 'lost gems' heading. To be honest, for example, how often have you seen photographs of Ann Street or Green's Village; the farms of Hay Mills; or, apart from our books, anything representing the city during the First World War?

Thanks to your efforts (along with a bit of help from us) we can go back to the era of trams and see, mainly for the first time, some of the more unusual happenings and high drama of the Second World War. Then, to complete the mix, the more familiar sights of post-war Birmingham. Actually, in one sense, that word 'familiar' isn't strictly true because, as with all our books, most of the items have never been seen before. So, prepare yourself for a lovely wallow in the world of yesterday!

Yours, in friendship,

Wholesale Meat Market, Cheapside, 5th July 1954.

Ann Street, with the Town Hall just visible, 1867.

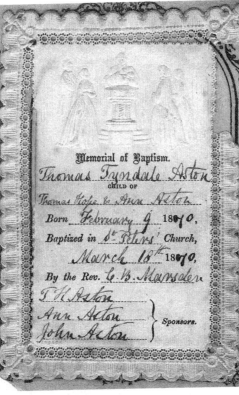

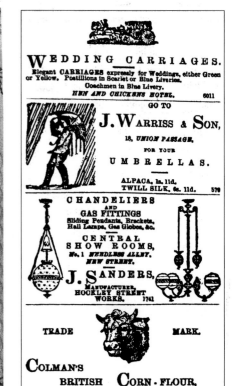

A court leading into The Gullet, between Stafford Street and Lichfield Street, c1872.

Back of 12/13 Upper Priory, 1872.

The Old Farriers Arms, Lichfield Street, Aston, 1880.

Green's Village/John Bright Street, 1880.

Malt Shovel Inn, Smallbrook Street/Horse Fair, 1882.

Mason College, Edmund Street, c1885.

Celebrating Queen Victoria's Jubilee, Cherry Street/Corporation Street, 21st June 1887. Rackhams (House of Fraser) is now on this site.

Queen's College, Paradise Street, 1889.

No. 10 Court, Cheapside, c1890.

Labelling cocoa essence packets, Cadbury's, 1890.

Sutton Street, Aston, c1890.

Marzipan making in Cadbury's Confectionery Room, 1890.

New Street, c1890.

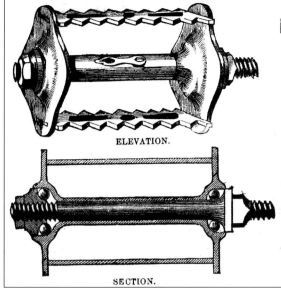

Heybarnes Farm, later to become part of Heybarnes Recreation Ground,
Hay Mills, c1895.

The opening cross-country run is about to start, from Muntz Street,
Small Heath, 1898.

Christ Church, 1899. By now, partially demolished, this was replaced
by Galloway's Corner which in turn, disappeared in 1970.
This area now forms part of Victoria Square.

BIRMINGHAM NOTES.

The Entertainment given by Anthony Diamond and Jabez White a big Success.

[BY OUR RESIDENT CORRESPONDENT.]

Larry Burns and his genial friend and adviser, Pat Moran, have left Birmingham, in which city they have made a whole host of friends. Each will carry with him any amount of good wishes, and, should they return, they can rest assured of a hearty welcome.

* *

Mr. Fred Jones, who presides over the Clements' Vaults, Newtown Row, Birmingham, is a valuable addition to the list of vocalists on the programme of smoking concerts. I hear that his services have been received by the choirmaster of a church in the neighbourhood.

* *

Anthony Diamond has secured the services of Jabez White, Charley Simpson, and Harry Tongue as assistants. His boxing academy at the rear of the "Green Lamp," Dale End, Birmingham, is being largely supported, and some likely lads will shortly emerge from Anthony's stable.

* *

The members of the Olympic Club are disappointed that there is no likelihood of a second match between Harry Greenfield and Larry Burns taking place in Birmingham. The young American has gained a host of friends during his stay in Birmingham, and he would have no difficulty in securing a substantial backing for a second trial against the Camden Town man. Charley Tilley is also red-hot on the trail of the latter, who, however, appear to be content to rest for a while on the laurels he recently won by beating Burns.

* *

The desire to accord Mr. Jack Brown, of Birmingham, a testimonial, is almost unanimous in the Midlands. Mr. Brown is one of the oldest supporters of the prize ring, and could be found in the corners of most of the fighters from Brum, when "things was things," to quote the expression of this great old sport. I have been deputed to look up a suitable place for the "ben" and was lucky enough to run across Mr. Harry Lyons, the genial manager of the Queen's Theatre, at the Olympic Club the other night who expressed his willingness to assist the movement in any way. A list of donations in aid of the movement has been opened; I shall be pleased to receive and acknowledge amounts, large or small, and cannot too strongly urge the claims of "one of the best" to the notice of those who admire one of the bull-dog breed who has fallen upon rough times.

* *

Anthony Diamond and Jabez White scored a decided success last Tuesday, at the Alexandra Hall, Hope Street, Birmingham. Boxers were so plentiful that the promoters could not find room for them in the dressing-room, and it was a difficult matter to pick out the best for the show. The room was packed with a company comprising some of the best supporters of boxing in the Midlands. Mr. Harry S. Cleveland, representing the POLICE GAZETTE, was master of ceremonies and refereed the contests, and Mr. Harry Knight, late of the Birmingham Amateur Boxing Club, held the watch. Harry Adams and Harry Lee, a couple of smart amateurs, fought a five-round draw, and the rest of the programme consisted of exhibition sparring. Charley Gifford proved in his spar with Francis Mole that he has the making of a really good lad at about 8 st. 10 lbs. The brothers Parrish gave only a moderate show. Ted Phillips and Jem Gough, on the other hand, satisfied the critics to the full. Their work was clear and hard and the verdict, "good lads both," met with general approval. Fred Warner and "Darkey" Edwards were cautious but clever; on the other hand Charley Simpson and Bill Bull were clever and lively. Anthony Diamond, who retains much of the science for which he was famous about a decade ago, made matters fairly interesting for Paddy Ryan, who some years back gained prominence as "Greenfield's Dummy." Harry Tongue, a much improved Birmingham boxer, took on an old opponent in C. Barratt, a youth from Cottonopolis. The ring was hardly large enough to give them a fair chance of showing their abilities, but enabled them to "make the fur fly" during the time they were in it. Jabez White and Harvey Checketts also "fought their battles o'er again." Their set-to was a really splendid exhibition of the business. Fred Reeves, in addition to being a smart boxer, is a clever second, and shared the duties of adviser with Tom Dunn.

Small Heath Park, with the imposing restaurant in the background, c1900.

Ladypool Road/Stratford Road, Sparkbrook, c1900.

Regent Row, off Warstone Lane (part of the Jewellery Quarter) c1900.

Weaver's hairdressing saloon, Coventry Road, Hay Mills, 1900.

Bull Ring area, Moat Row/Jamaica Row, 1901.

At work in the bedstead factory of Fisher Brown & Bayley Ltd.,
Lionel Street, 1901.

The statue of Queen Victoria on the day of her funeral, Victoria Square, 2nd February 1901.

Kings Norton Union Workhouse, Raddlebarn Road, Selly Oak, 1903.

Beaty Reynolds, outside Mr Burgess' hardware shop, Bristol Road, Selly Oak, 7th July 1903.

The old cottages, The Fordrough, Hay Mills, 1903. The pump handle has been removed and the new tap is in use.

Springfield Road, Sparkhill, 1905.

Highbury Hall, the family home of the Chamberlain family, c1905.
The house was built in 1878. The photograph shows Joseph and
his eldest son, Austen.

Chamberlain Square, 1905.

Steelhouse Lane, c1906.

Sir Johns Road, Selly Oak, 1908.

Great Western Arcade, c1908.

Stoney Lane, Yardley, 1908.

The Master Bakers' and Confectioners' of Great Britain and Ireland
visit to Cadbury's, 30th June 1908.

20

Sycamore Road, Bournville, c1910.

Fresh milk on its way for Cadbury's chocolate, 1910.

Florence's Farm, Coventry Road, Hay Mills, c1910.

Frederick and William Florence, Hay Hall Farm,
Hay Hall Road, Tyseley, c1910.

21

Proclamation of His Majesty, KING GEORGE 5th by the Lord Mayor of Birmingham, May 10th. 1910.

Edwards & Co. Publishers, New Street, Birmingham

Ye Olde Swan, Washwood Heath, c1910.

High Street, Kings Heath, Spring 1910.

Bull Ring, c1910.

Ladder drill for Aston Fire Brigade, c1910.

Small Heath Fire Brigade, Bordesley Green Fire Station, c1910.

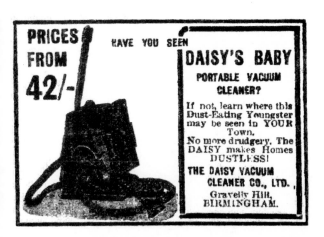

Selly Manor, on its original site in Bournbrook Road, Selly Oak, 1911. It was later moved to Bournville.

Holders Arms, Washington St, 1911.

People's Hall, Oak Tree Lane, Selly Oak, 1911. It also doubled as the Selly Oak Picturedome.

Staff Room, King Edward VI Grammar School, Handsworth, 1911.

25

Saltley Picture Palace, Alum Rock Road, 1912.

TITANIC SINKS FOUR HOURS AFTER HITTING ICEBERG; 866 RESCUED BY CARPATHIA, PROBABLY 1250 PERISH; ISMAY SAFE, MRS. ASTOR MAYBE, NOTED NAMES MISSING

14.4.12

Tilling-Stevens' double decker bus at the Bear Hotel terminus, Sandon Road, Edgbaston, 1913.

Blakesley Hall, Blakesley Road, Yardley, 1914.

Class 5B, King Edward's Grammar School for Girls, Handsworth, 1914.

Senior Class, Hope Street School, Highgate, 1914.

Birmingham City Battalions parade in Victoria Square, just prior to the outbreak of war, 1914.

Recruiting Parade passes The Don (clothes dealers), Corporation Street, 1914.

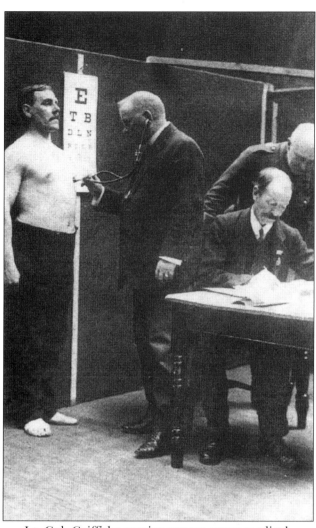

Lt. Col. Griffiths carries out an army medical,
Curzon Hall, Suffolk Street, 1914.

Territorials engaged in annual rifle training practice using
moving targets, on film, 1914.

Due to the absence of men, women volunteer for street cleaning
jobs, 1st World War.

Recruiting Parade, Saltley Viaduct, 1914.

THE LUSITANIA TORPEDOED BY GERMAN PIRATES

Cunard's Mammoth Liner That Cost £1,250,000 Sunk in Eight Minutes—1,918 Souls on Board.

DASH OF RESCUE SHIPS IN REPLY TO "S.O.S." CALL—MANY LIVES SAVED

OFFICIAL NOTICE OF MURDER PLAN.

Huns' Warning Threat to Passengers

Local Defence Volunteers at camp, 1915.

THERE IS STILL A PLACE IN THE LINE FOR YOU

THIS SPACE IS RESERVED FOR A FIT MAN

Will you fill it?

Boys Come over here you're wanted

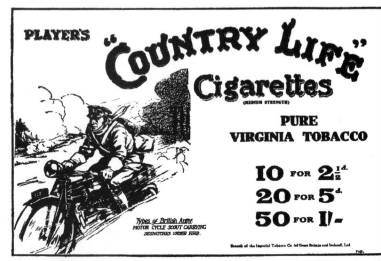

PLAYER'S "COUNTRY LIFE" Cigarettes (MEDIUM STRENGTH)

PURE VIRGINIA TOBACCO

10 FOR 2¼
20 FOR 5ᵈ
50 FOR 1ᐟ—

Oak Tree Lane, Selly Oak, 1915.

Rudge Whitworth Ladies F.C., 1917.

Comfort for the troops, New Street Station, c1917.

31

Temporary accommodation for the military, Colmore Road Council School, Kings Heath, c1917.

MY ANSWER TO MICHAELIS: By MR. BOTTOMLEY

SUNDAY · PICTORIAL

LATEST CERTIFIED CIRCULATION MORE THAN TWO MILLION COPIES WEEKLY

| No. 124. | Registered at the G.P.O. as a Newspaper. | SUNDAY, JULY 22, | The Paper with " The Daily Mirror " Behind It. | 1917 |

32 NEW V C.s BESTOWED BY THE KING—HONOUR FOR HERO'S BABY

Wounded soldiers recover at the Earl of Plymouth's estate, Barnt Green 1917.

Mr. Churchill's Return.

WE welcome the return of Mr. Churchill to office as Minister of Munitions. He will revitalise the office by his driving power and forceful energy. There will be a punch in his portfolio. Mr. Churchill has the war mind. He is a good hater of the enemy.

A certain section of the Unionist Party complains that the Premier has entirely altered the complexion of the Government by his new appointments. The suggestion is that Mr. Walter Long and others would not have accepted office if they had anticipated the re-entry of Mr. Churchill. But now is not the time to stir the ashes of party. All should realise this.

There is no need for any of us to be alarmed when we read prophecies of disaster to the national cause because once upon a time Mr. Churchill left the Conservative party and because Mr. Montagu happens to be a Liberal in politics. These prophecies are the works of prophets with their faces turned backwards. And our business is not with them, but with the enemy and with the future.

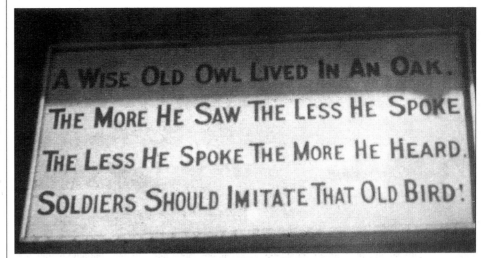

A WISE OLD OWL LIVED IN AN OAK.
THE MORE HE SAW THE LESS HE SPOKE
THE LESS HE SPOKE THE MORE HE HEARD.
SOLDIERS SHOULD IMITATE THAT OLD BIRD!

We're both needed to serve the Guns!

FILL UP THE RANKS!
PILE UP THE MUNITIONS!

Take the coal OFF the fire

when you go to bed, or when you no longer need to use the room rake out the fire. Be just as careful to turn out the fire as you are to turn off the gas.

The coal you save to-day will start your fire to-morrow. Put the coals under the grate, and if they don't go out easily throw a little water over them.

Next morning pick the cinders carefully out of the debris under the grate. Everything will burn again except the ash dust. Use a sifter if you have one. The cinders saved will give you many bright glowing fires.

The Coal you go without is forging the key to
VICTORY

Issued by the Coal News Dept., Board of Trade, Holborn Viaduct, E.C.1.

Munitions' workers at Charles Smith & Son, Deritend Bridge Works, 1917.

Military parade preparations in Victoria Square, 1918.

Birmingham 1st City Battalion, 1918.

Taylor & Challen Ltd. (engineers), Livery Street, 1920.

Cost of the War in Gold

Many efforts have been made to ascertain what was the total direct cost of the Great War in money expressly expended upon it. The following figures, collected from various sources, indicate the approximate direct expenditure of the chief participants:

	£
Great Britain	6,418,000,000
France	5,200,000,000*
Russia	5,060,000,000*
German Empire	8,300,000,000*
Italy	2,400,000,000*
Austria-Hungary	4,100,000,000*
U.S.A.	2,600,000,000*
Other countries and neutrals ..	1,370,000,000*

*These are expressed in £ sterling at par rate of exchange.

The greater part of these figures were obtained from the speech of the late Sir Edward Holden at the annual meeting of the London City and Midland Bank of January 29, 1919, and from "The Statesman's Year Book," while a few are estimated from the carefully selected information in Professor Bogart's book "Preliminary Economic Studies of the War." Other figures are taken from "British Finance 1914-21," by A. W. Kirkaldy.

Britain's daily expenditure on the War between certain periods was officially given as follows. The figures include loans to her Dominions and Allies:

	£
Oct. 8 to Dec. 9, 1916	5,714,000
April 1 to May 5, 1917	7,457,000
April 1 to Sept. 29, 1917 ..	6,648,000
Nov. 1, 1917, to Jan. 9, 1918 ..	7,517,000
Nov. 1, 1917, to Feb. 9, 1918 ..	6,107,000
April 1 to June 8, 1918 ..	6,848,000
April 1 to Nov. 9, 1918 ..	7,443,000

The following table shows the amount of money spent by Great Britain during each year on the various services:

	1914-15	1915-16	1916-17	1917-18	1918-19
	£	£	£	£	£
Army	211,900,000	526,700,000	587,800,000	725,800,000	824,700,000
Navy	51,700,000	205,700,000	209,800,000	227,400,000	334,100,000
Air Force				2,500,000	85,400,000
Munitions	700,000	224,600,000	504,900,000	641,000,000	458,300,000
Railways & Canals	6,800,000	5,900,000	16,900,000	26,400,000	49,600,000
Shipping ..	—	—	8,100,000	110,900,000	100,400,000
Food	9,700,000	7,300,000	22,400,000	79,300,000	41,500,000
Pensions ..	100,000	2,200,000	7,800,000	23,700,000	46,600,000
Miscellaneous ..	4,000,000	95,300,000	60,600,000	106,600,000	96,700,000
Loans to Allies & Dominions ..	51,800,000	316,000,000	544,700,000	488,300,000	264,600,000
Total	346,700,000	1,383,700,000	1,963,000,000	2,431,900,000	2,301,900,000

The total of 8,417 millions is considerably higher than the one previously given, but this is due to certain deductions. In the former the loans to Allies and Dominions are not included, as it was thought they would be repaid. The normal cost of the navy and the army during the War years was also deducted, this being a sum of about £500,000,000. With these two deductions the two totals are very much the same—something like £6,500,000,000. On the other hand, some authorities put the cost of the War at a very much higher figure than 6,000 or 7,000 millions sterling. For instance, Mr. Edgar Crammond, addressing the Institute of Bankers in 1920, added to it a further 5,200 millions made up as follows:

	£
Capitalized cost of war pensions	1,300,000,000
Money borrowed abroad	1,300,000,000
Sale of British securities abroad	1,000,000,000
Shipping and other trading losses	1,600,000,000
	5,200,000,000

Whichever estimate is accepted, it is certain that the National Debt of Great Britain was increased by something over £7,000,000,000. This is shown by the following figures:

	£
April 1, 1914	651,000,000
March 31, 1920	7,882,000,000
Increase, 1914-19	7,231,000,000

NAVAL AND MERCHANT SHIPPING LOSSES

Naval	British	Allied	German
Capital Ships	16	12	2
Cruisers and Light cruisers	25	17	
Destroyers and Torpedo boats	75	62	123
Submarines	54	35	200
Miscellaneous	899	160	165
Total	1069	286	513

Merchant Tonnage		
Year	British	World Total
1914	241,201	312,672
1915	855,721	1,307,996
1916	1,237,634	2,327,326
1917	3,729,785	6,235,878
1918	1,604,749	2,666,942
Total	7,759,090	12,850,811

New Street, c1920.

Birmingham City Prize Band, c1920.

Hay Mills' Brass Band, 1920.

Neville Chamberlain (centre) prepares to open the first permanent branch of the Birmingham Municipal Bank, Stratford Road, Sparkbrook, 25th July 1921.

Greet School, Warwick Road, 1922.

A Child's Advertisement to Children.

My Daddy brings me home a real Picture Newspaper of my very own every Thursday, "THE BOYS & GIRLS' PICTURE NEWSPAPER." Nearly everything is told in pictures, with stories of the important things that are happening all over the world, and I can understand every word of it because it's all explained so nicely. I simply love it. Daddy says it's a splendid thing for Boys and Girls to know what is going on around them and making history. Then there are wonderful tales, all kinds of lovely articles, and anecdotes, and prizes, and—oh, everything you can think of! Why don't you ask your Daddy to buy it for you?

Albert Road/War Lane, Harborne, 1922.

Power Presses, Joseph Lucas Ltd., Great King Street, Hockley, 1922.

Joe Pinfold crosses the River Cole, in flood, near to Hob Moor Lane,
Hay Mills, c1923.

The Oak Cinema, Bristol Road, Selly Oak, 1923.

Ansells deliver to Anderton Park Road, Sparkbrook, 1923.

39

Lawley Street Goods' Station St John Ambulance Division, 1925.

Crowds gather for the opening of the Hall of Memory, 4th July 1925.
The ceremony was performed by Prince Arthur of Connaught.

Kings Norton and District Schools
Sports' Association

FOURTH COMBINED

Athletic Festival

UNDER A.A.A. RULES.

〜〜〜〜〜〜〜〜〜〜〜〜〜〜〜

Wednesday, June 30th, 1926,

to be held on the

Central Secondary School Ground,

Elmdon Road, Selly Park,

(by kind permission of the Head Master.)

Doug Copley, landlord of the Wagon & Horses, Coventry Road, Sheldon, 1926.

The City of Birmingham Salvage Dept., Rotton Park Street, 1926.

Refreshment Room, Platform 7, Snow Hill Station, 1926.

All Saints C. of E. School, All Saints Street, Winson Green, 1926.

Raddlebarn Athletic F.C., winners of the Aston Villa Cup, 1926/27.

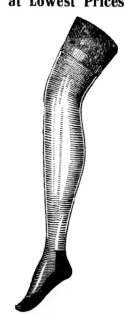

Platform 5, Snow Hill Station, July 1927.

Workers from Dunlop Rubber Co. Ltd. on a trip to Jacob's Ladder, Cheddar, 1927.

Preparing to leave for a trip from Spring Hill to Blackpool, 1927.

A trip to Evesham for the men from the Park Tavern, High Street, Aston, c1927.

Edgbaston Reservoir, 1928.

George Cadbury bowls the first wood at the opening of the Weoley Hill Sports' Centre, 28th April 1928.

League winners, Steward Street School Old Boys' XI, 1927/28.

Kings Norton Girls' Secondary School, June 1928.

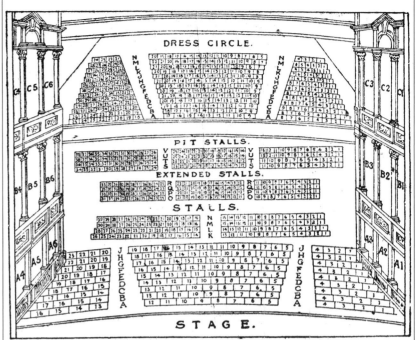

Stable lads, drivers and blacksmiths, Top Yard, H.P. Sauce Ltd., Aston, 1928.

Joseph Lucas Ltd., Great King Street, Hockley, c1928.

The cast of "Aladdin", Alexandra Theatre, December 1928.

Villa Cross Picture House, Heath Road, Handsworth, 1928.

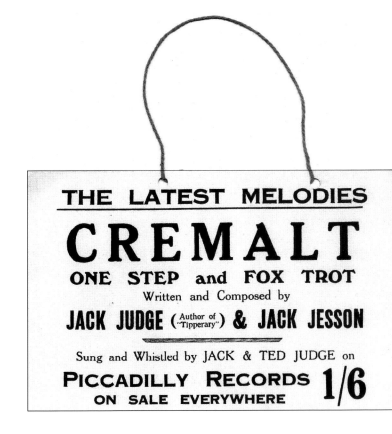
Philips & Son (grocers), Bloomsbury Street, Nechells, c1928.

Shirley Road, the site of Acocks Green Library, 1928.

Kings Road, Hay Mills, 1929.

The General Hospital, Steelhouse Lane, 1929.

Road repairs underneath the railway bridge in Brighton Road, Balsall Heath, 18th September 1929.

Group 2, St Mathias' School, Wheeler Street, Hockley, 1929.

Corporation Street, 1930.

Another of those mystery items! What was the occasion? Why would over 50 people, of various ages, gather outside the Plume of Feathers in Miles Street, Small Heath, sometime in 1930?

Corporation Street, with Lewis's on the left, Summer, 1930.

The after-effects of the tornado, Wordsworth Road/Coventry Road, Small Heath, 14th June 1931.

Farm Park, Sampson Road, Sparkbrook, 27th May 1932.

The view from Birmingham University clock tower, looking towards the Bristol Road, 5th July 1932.

Second Form pupils, St James' Junior School, Brewery Street,
Handsworth, 1932.

Congreve Street/Edmund Street, 1933.

Tyburn Road Bus Repair Works, 1933.

Children in search of water during the great drought, Summer 1934.

The Orient cinema, High Street, Aston, 1934.

54 Joseph Chamberlain's library at Highbury, Moor Green, 1934.

A BUSY DAY FOR THE PRINCE.

PROGRAMME OF VISIT TO BIRMINGHAM.

THE NEW HOSPITALS CENTRE.

FOUNDATION-STONE TO BE LAID.

INSPECTION OF SLUM CLEARANCE AREAS.

The Prince of Wales will fulfil a number of engagements in Birmingham on Tuesday. From shortly before 11 a.m. his Royal Highness will be busily engaged until nearly five o'clock in the afternoon.

The primary purpose of the visit is the foundation-stone laying of the administration block on the new Hospitals Centre site at Edgbaston. The Prince has consented to receive gifts of £100 and upwards to the Appeal Fund of the new Hospitals Centre. A number of promises of cheques has already been received.

This ceremony will be followed by the cutting of the first sod of the new Medical School of Birmingham University.

Luncheon will be taken at the Council House. Several occupational centres in various parts of the city will be visited in the morning and afternoon, and a tour will be made of some of the slum-clearance areas.

Bennett Ashton and his band, 1935.

The Town Hall is renovated, 1935.

The new frontage is underway, Alexandra Theatre, John Bright Street, 1935.

First try out for the floodlighting, Chamberlain Square, 3rd May 1935.

Exhibition of work, Ryland Road School, Erdington, 1936.

Cyclo Gear Co., Potters Hill, Aston, c1936.

Cromwell Hall outing to Marston Green, c1936.

Prize-winning line-up of railway delivery men and their horses, New Street Station, 1936.

Smithfield Market, 9th April 1936.

Union Chambers, Temple Row, c1936.

Dalton Street (off Bull Street), 1936.

The new swimming baths are almost completed, Bristol Road South, Northfield, 1936.

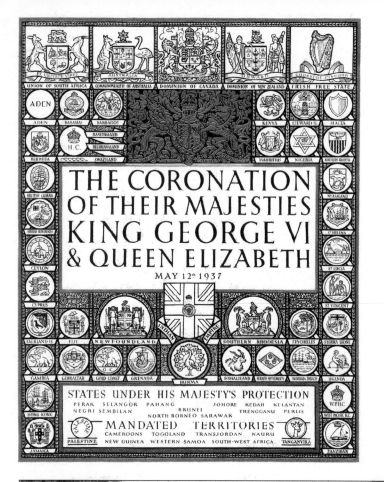

THE CORONATION
OF THEIR MAJESTIES
KING GEORGE VI
& QUEEN ELIZABETH

MAY 12th 1937

STATES UNDER HIS MAJESTY'S PROTECTION

PERAK   SELANGOR   PAHANG   JOHORE   KEDAH   KELANTAN
NEGRI SEMBILAN   BRUNEI   TRENGGANU   PERLIS
           NORTH BORNEO   SARAWAK

MANDATED TERRITORIES

CAMEROONS   TOGOLAND   TRANSJORDAN   NAURU
NEW GUINEA   WESTERN SAMOA   SOUTH-WEST AFRICA

CORONATION DECORATIONS 1937
CORPORATION ST.   BIRMINGHAM.

CORONATION 1937 DECORATIONS   THE CITY ARCADE BIRMINGHAM

Decorated for the Coronation of King George VI and Queen Elizabeth, New Street, 12th May 1937.

Raddlebarn Road School, Kings Norton Schools' athletic champions, Selly Oak, 1937.

Slade Lane, Hall Green, 1937.

A rare shot of Crooked Lane, taken from Union Passage towards Martineau Street, 1937.

Chamberlain Place, 7th June 1938.

Weoley Hill, Weoley Castle, 1938.

A ramble on the Lickey Hills, 1938.

Cannon Hill Park, 1938.

Week-End Wireless

MIDLAND—1,013 Kilocycles, 296.2 Metres

To-day (Friday).—**10.15 a.m.,** The daily service ; **10.30,** Weather forecast for farmers and shipping ; **10.45,** Organ from the Gaumont Palace Cinema, Birmingham ; **11.15,** Northern Ireland Orchestra, with Elsie McCullough (soprano) : **12.15 p.m.,** Wynford Reynolds Octet ; **12.45,** Marjorie Bates (piano) ; **1.15,** Gramophone ; **1.45,** B.B.C. Theatre Organ ; **2.15,** Empire Orchestra, with Antonio Brosa (violin) ; **3.15,** Orchestra from the Carlton Hotel ; **3.50,** Talk— " The History of Jazz " ; **4.20,** " Oliver Twist " (Part 2), from the novel by Charles Dickens ; **5.0,** Children's Hour ; **6.0,** Maddison String Trio ; **6.20,** Eugene Pini and his Tango Orchestra, with Diana Clare ; **7.0,** News ; **7.20,** Announcements ; **7.30,** Carols by the choir (from Peterborough Cathedral) ; **8.0,** " Goodwill Towards Men "—Christmas Eve anthology of verse, prose, and story from the Bible and the writings of various authors ; **8.30,** Louis Levy and his Symphony ; **9.10,** B.B.C. Orchestra, with Heddle Nash (tenor) ; **10.0,** News, sport and topical talks ; **10.25,** Dance music from the Astoria Dance Salon ; **11.30,** Late news ; **11.40 to 12.0,** Gramophone.

Christmas Day.—**10.30 a.m.,** Weather forecast for farmers and shipping ; **12.0 noon,** Northern Orchestra ; **1.0 p.m.,** Alec Rowley and Edgar Moy (two pianos) and Ernest Butcher (baritone) ; **2.0,** B.B.C. Theatre Organ ; **2.30,** Talk—" Practical Cats " ; **2.45,** B.B.C. Military Band ; **3.0,** The King's Christmas message to home and Empire (from Sandringham) ; **3.15,** B.B.C. Military Band ; **3.30,** Cabaret from the Headland Hotel, Newquay ; **4.0,** " The Wondrous Lamp of Al-Addin," a pantomime ; **5.0,** Children's Hour ; **6.0,** Orchestra from the New Hippodrome Theatre, Coventry ; **6.40,** " Sport in the Midlands," with eyewitness account of the League match between Wolverhampton Wanderers and West Bromwich Albion ; **6.50,** Sports bulletin ; **7.0,** " Schubert," played by the Alfred Cave String Quartet ; **7.25,** Christmas stories—" The Shirt " and " Dunworthy 13 " ; **8.10,** " The Bartered Bride " (Act III) (from the National Theatre, Prague) ; **9.0,** News, sport and topical talks ; **9.10,** National ; **9.20,** B.B.C. Theatre Orchestra ; **10.0,** George Elrick and his Music Makers ; **10.40,** Roy Fox and his Band ; **11.20 to 12.0,** Dance music from Grosvenor House, Park Lane.

Sunday.—**4.0 p.m.,** Hans Scharlig and the St. Moritz Yodellers ; **4.20,** Talk—" Music of the Week " ; **4.30** " For the Children " ; **5.0,** Orchestre Raymonde, with chorus ; **5.50,** Talk—" Watching Birds in Winter " ; **6.5,** John Allen (baritone) ; **6.25,** " Three Strangers," a play adapted from the story by Thomas Hardy ; **7.0,** Birmingham Hippodrome Orchestra ; **8.0,** National ; **8.45,** Appeal on behalf of the North Staffordshire Royal Infirmary ; **8.50,** News ; **9.5,** London Symphony Orchestra, with Lisa Perli (soprano) and Roy Henderson (baritone) ; **10.30,** Epilogue.

Kings Norton Church, 15th May 1938.

Treasure Trove, Pershore Road, Cotteridge, 1938.

Dudley Road, with Icknield Port Road on the right, Winston Green, c1938.

Soho Road/Grove Lane, 1938.

Aston Street, with the Central Fire Station on the left, c1938.

St Pauls' C. of E. School, Vincent Street, Balsall Heath, c1938.

Prime Minister, Neville Chamberlain, returns to England, after signing what turned out to be the worthless Munich agreement with Hitler on 29th September 1938. Mr Chamberlain had been Lord Mayor of Birmingham from 1915/17.

Great crowds cheer Premier home and hear him say:

"IT IS PEACE IN OUR TIME, YOU MAY SLEEP QUIETLY"

Billy Forrest's Sunday Rhythm Club, Co-op Hall, Stratford Road, Sparkhill, 1938. Billy is seen shaking hands with jazz trombonist, George Chisholm.

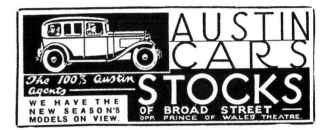

A dancing display for the King and Queen at the Town Hall, 1st March 1939.

Sandbags, placed around the Town Hall in an attempt to avoid possible bomb damage, September 1939.

City children wait to be evacuated to the countryside, September 1939.

1940

Civil Defence rehearsal, at a local school, 1940. For obvious reasons precise details were seldom given, particularly during the early war years.

Gas detectors have been erected in some streets, 1940. They were coated with a substance that changed colour when gas was about.

The staff and families from Hudson & Son (letterpress & lithographic printers), Edmund Street, prepare for a day trip, c1940.

As a result of the blackout this car finished up on a roundabout, 1940.

A girl from the Auxiliary Territorial Service is cleaning a rifle, using a pull-through, 1940.

ARP personnel on parade, watched by members of the Fire Service, the Home Guard, the Regular Army and the general public, Calthorpe Park, Balsall Heath, 30th March 1940.

The results of a high explosive bomb on Edmund Street,
22nd November 1940.

The premises of Jarrett, Rainsford and Laughton Ltd.
(hairpin mnfrs.), Kent Street, demolished in the blitz
of 20th November 1940.

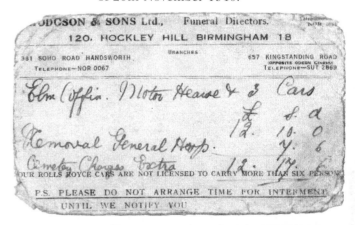

An Anderson shelter, in Small Heath, saves several lives,
September 1940.

Livery Street, with Snow Hill Station on the right, 1940.

The King, accompanied by the Lord Mayor, Ald Wilfrid Martineau and Regional Commissioner, Lord Dudley, see bomb-damaged Aston for themselves, 12th December 1940.

Pigeons are often used for sending messages from aircraft and this one is being placed in a metal container in case the plane is brought down in the sea, 1941.

Changing Face !

Yesterday it was a block of offices. Today it's a mass of rubble. A man has got to be prepared for changes these days. Thank goodness something is always the same maybe the grocers' boys couldn't resist helping themselves to a few drops of H.P. Sauce.

The Home Guard operates a road block, at the city limits, 1941. He turned out to be one of their own and was allowed through.

The Home Guard practise scaling the walls of a bombed-out building in Sparkhill, using toggle ropes, 1942.

'Walkie-Talkie' radio equipment put into use by a member of the National Fire Service, 1944.

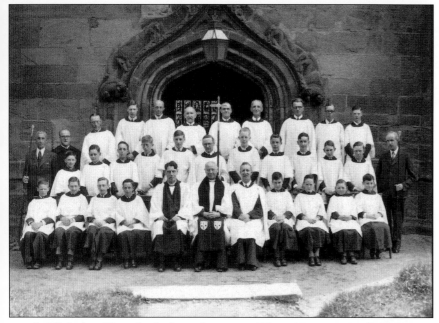
St Nicholas Church choir and servers, Kings Norton, April 1944.

Members of the ATS sort parcels and post at an Army Postal Depot in the city, 1944.

Northfield Parish Magazine

No. 515. **DECEMBER, 1944.** **Price—2d.**

CLERGY—

The Rev. REGINALD A. HAYSOM, M.A., Chaplain R.A.F.—On Active Service.
The Rev. G. F. D. PITTS, M.A., (in charge) 20, Staplehall Road, Northfield. Tel. PRIory 2469.

CHURCHWARDENS.—
Mr. A. SAGE, Ryland House, Northfield, and
Mr. S. W. H. DAVEY, 61, Bunbury Road, Northfield.

ORGANIST AND CHOIRMASTER — Mr. J. H. GREENWOOD, 91, Quarry Lane, Northfield.

SECRETARY OF THE CHURCH FUND.—Mr. A. A. L. BANKS, 21, Chelston Road, Northfield.

SECRETARY PAROCHIAL CHURCH COUNCIL—
Miss M. J. BANTON, 6, Woodland Road, Northfield, 31.

VERGER.—Mr. J. WITHERS, 29, Church Hill, Northfield.
SACRISTAN—Mr. H. W. W. GUMBLEY, 22, Hemyock Road, Selly Oak.

74

A TRIBUTE TO

OUR

WOMENFOLK

THEY ALSO

SERVED

N°1 ~ 17/18

PLATOON

BHM 22

To Louis Camillis

1940 - 1944

13th DECEMBER 1944

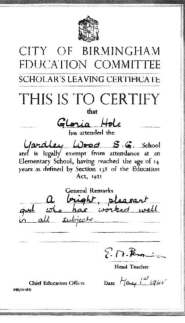

Officers and NCO's of the Birmingham Auxiliary Bomb Disposal Unit, May 1945.

GERMANY CAPITULATES!

Today is VE Day: "Complete and Crushing Victory"

GERMAN NATION TOLD OF SURRENDER
Address on this

King Thanks Eisenhower
Crushing Victory

GERMANS IN NORWAY HAVE SURRENDERED
FIGHTING CONTINUES IN

VE-DAY FLAGS

PREPARATIONS FOR CELEBRATIONS

FLOODLIGHTS IN CITY CENTRE

Preparations for decorating cities and towns in Britain were started at an early hour to-day

In Birmingham the civic authorities were preparing to floodlight the Council House, the Hall of Memory, and the Cathedral, and beflag the Town Hall, but business houses, hotels, shops, and the rank and file of the citizens seemed shy of displaying their relief at the end of hostilities in Europe.

A BASIC petrol ration, substantially the same as in the United States, and freely at the disposal of owners of cars and motor-cycles, will be introduced within 30 days, said Mr. Churchill in the House of Commons yesterday.

The petrol ration books can be collected from post offices from May 16. It is expected that the date on which they will become valid will be June 1. The monthly allowance will be:

Cars up to 9 h.p.	....	4 gallons
10 to 13 h.p.	....	5 „
14 to 19 h.p.	....	6 „
20 h.p. and over	....	7 „

Motor-cycles: 2 to 3, according to cylinder capacity.

Roughly this means that each car-owner will be able to do about 120 miles of pleasure motoring a month.

VE Day Party, Franklin Street, Winson Green, 8th May 1945.

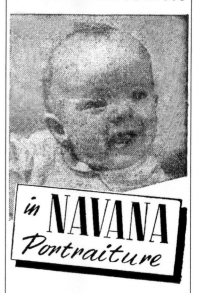

Miss Poynter's Physical Culture Club, Botanical Gardens, June 1945.

DAILY EXPRESS

No. 14,101   Lighting-up: 9.24 pm to 4.45 am   WEDNESDAY AUGUST 15 1945   Weather: Transitory rain   One Penny

The full dramatic story of the last day of war

PEACE ON EARTH

*Japan accepts Allied surrender terms :
Attlee gives the news at midnight*

DAWN FESTIVITIES
———◆———

BIRMINGHAM & MIDLANDS GO GAY EARLY

IN the bright morning sun the almost empty streets in the centre of the city showed remarkably few signs of the overnight revelry. The statues round the Town Hall, however, had received attention and seemed to be carrying their peace-paint with an injured air. King Edward VII had a red nose and flushed cheeks and Queen Victoria had been given a liberal touching up with lipstick and rouge. The masterpiece of re-decoration was in Chamberlain Place, where Josiah Mason sat in front of his college in a positively mediæval make-up. His face had been carefully painted red, leaving the grey stone hair untouched, and he held on his knees one of those red signs reading "No Entry. One-Way Street." His right hand was broken, revealing the always dis-illusioning fact that these solid-looking statues are hollow. Across the way his neighbour, John Skirrow Wright, evidently had put up a better fight and had escaped defacement at the cost of a broken nose and missing finger.

City Road Day Nursery, Edgbaston, 19th March 1946.

Bloomsbury School, Lingard Street, Saltley, 10th April 1946.

Because of terrible weather the Army had to be called in to deliver coal to Saltley Gasworks, 17th February 1947.

GEC Works at Witton re-opens after the big freeze of 1947.

Management and staff, Stirchley Pavilion, 1947.

Kings Norton Library, Pershore Road South, 1948.

Victoria Square, 1949.

Metallurgy Laboratory Technicians, Birmingham University, c1949.

79

A tram travelling in the opposite direction to the one-way system, at the junction of Bull Street and Corporation Street, 1st July 1949.

Watford Road, Cotteridge, 1949.

Bull Street, seen from under the canopy of Grey's (Edward Grey Ltd, ladies outfitters, drapers, etc.), 1950.

Colmore Row, 1950.

Cannon Hill Park, 1950.

A disaster at Hill-Ouston Co. Ltd. (table glass mnfrs.), Woodbridge Road, Moseley, 12th May 1950.

A typical lunch hour scene in the grounds of St Philip's churchyard, looking towards Colmore Row, 24th April 1951.

Kings Norton Youth Fellowship, Kings Norton Cinema, July 1951.

D. E. BENNETT

Dave Bennett, from Rednal Road, Kings Norton, 1951. Sadly, he was killed in the Swiss Grand Prix the following year.

Another collection of equipment from Cyclo Gear Co. Ltd., Victoria Road, Aston, 1952.

City Road Infants' School, Edgbaston, 1952.

Needless Alley, c1953.

A group of prize-winning nurses at the Queen Elizabeth Hospital,
Edgbaston, 1954.

Aston Road North, 1954.

One of the city's oldest buildings, The Grey House, Union Street, c1954. Fyfe & Grey were dealers in foreign stamps.

Radio Luxembourg take over the Aston Hippodrome for one of their programmes, 6th November 1955. The compere (left) is Jack Watson and the contestants are soling and heeling shoes!

Principal girl, Jean Colquhoun, as 'Josepha', is targeted by the chorus of "White Horse Inn", Hippodrome, 19th December 1955.

Just prior to demolition, Clifford Street, Lozells, 1956.

Survivors of the Birmingham City Battalions (1914/18) lay a wreath at the memorial in St Martin's Church, 4th June 1957.

Dale End, from High Street, April 1958.

Bull Ring, with the front entrance to the Market Hall on the left, February 1959.

Cranes' music shop is demolished, Upper Priory/Corporation Street, February 1960.

Dr Johnson's Passage, showing a glimpse of Grey's, Bull Street, 23rd September 1960.

St Alban's School F.C., Dymoke Street, Balsall Heath, 1960/1. They were the Divisional Championship Winners.

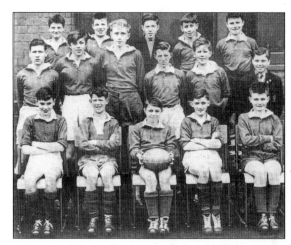

George Dixon Grammar School Rugby XV, Edgbaston, c1960.

High Street, Saltley, 20th January 1961.

The actress, Dame Sybil Thorndyke, launches the campaign to collect funds for the Birmingham Council for Old People, 27th March 1961. Her first donation came from Miss Frew, of Bristol Road, with the Appeals Chairman, Ald J R Balmer, in attendance.

School leavers' service, St Martin's Church, Bull Ring, 15th December 1961.

American pop idol, Brenda Lee, visits Summer Lane School, Aston, 7th May 1962. The previous night she'd appeared at the Town Hall.

Christmas shoppers at Grey's, Bull Street, 15th December 1962.

High Street, Erdington, 1963.

The building of the Catholic Church of St John Fisher is underway, West Heath, 1963. Rednal Road goes north through the centre of the photograph.

Members of the Golden Cross OAP Fund about to leave Metchley Lane, Harborne, for a day's outing to the Cotswolds, 8th July 1964.

The Creatours, semi-pro winners of the South Birmingham Beat Contest, 1964.